Wild Boars

Wild Boars

by Darrel Nicholson/photographs by Craig Blacklock

A Carolrhoda Nature Watch Book

Carolrhoda Books, Inc./Minneapolis

Till Hannele ja Marija:

"En liika omin lihoini
liikun Luojani lihoilla"
           —Kalevala

The publisher wishes to thank Dr. Marion Marshall-Nimis for her assistance with this book.

The author wishes to thank the following people for their help with this book: Sandra Sevre; Melvin Neuvonen; Police Commissioner Werner Franke, Hildesheim, West Germany; Dr. Reginald H. Barrett, University of California at Berkeley; Dr. Björn Kurtén, University of Helsinki.

LIBRARY OF CONGRESS CATALOGING-IN-PUBLICATION DATA

Nicholson, Darrel.
  Wild boars.

  "A Carolrhoda nature watch book."
  Includes index.
  Summary: Describes the physical characteristics, habits, natural environment, and relationship to humans of the wild boar.
  1. Wild boar—Juvenile literature. [1. Wild boar.
2. Pigs] I. Blacklock, Craig, ill. II. Title.
QL737.U58N53   1987   599.73′4   87-677
ISBN 0-87614-308-7 (lib. bdg.)

Manufactured in the United States of America

1 2 3 4 5 6 7 8 9 10 97 96 95 94 93 92 91 90 89 88 87

When we think of animals that have the intelligence and the temperament to work well with humans, dogs are usually the first to come to mind. In Hildesheim, West Germany, however, some people might think first of wild boars. With their ferocious and ungainly appearance, wild boars seem rather unsuited to being trained. Nevertheless, the chief commissioner of police in Hildesheim, Werner Franke, has trained a female wild boar named Luise to search outdoors for buried drugs and explosives. According to Franke, wild boars are ideally suited to be trained for this work because they easily form attachments to people. In addition, Franke points out that wild boars have a good memory, an amazingly keen sense of smell, and a high energy level that enables them to dig for long periods of time. Luise has found items buried as much as 3 feet (about 1 meter) underground.

Wild boars' intelligence and their potential usefulness to people are qualities that are not commonly associated with these animals. The wild boar is known as a ferocious fighter, a reputation it earns when it is attacked or cornered by animals or people. Wild boars will also fight to defend their piglets and to win a mate. The lesser-known facts of this animal's family life, however, reveal a relatively peaceful existence. With its keen senses of smell and hearing, its speed, and its intelligence, the wild boar is hard to follow in the wild. For this reason, few studies have been done on the family life of wild boars. The wild boars in this book were studied and photographed in a semienclosed farm

near New York Mills, Minnesota, a small town in the west central part of the state. The first pair of wild boars for the farm was caught on islands off the coast of California and shipped to Minnesota. Groups of wild boars are not otherwise found in Minnesota's wilderness areas.

The word boar has two meanings. It is the word used to refer to a male pig of any **species**, or kind, that is able to **breed**. The word boar can also be used as a specific species name to refer to both male and female wild boars *(Sus scrofa).*

There are two **families**, or groups, of piglike animals, the Peccaries (scientific family name Tayssuidae) and the Old World Pigs (scientific family name Suidae), or true pigs. Wild boars, members of the Suidae family, are just one of many different species of wild pigs. Wild boars first lived in Asia, but they eventually came to live in Europe, Great Britain, parts of northern Africa, Japan, and some far eastern islands through the intervention of humans and through the animals' own wanderings. The animals that descend from these wild boars are called Eurasian wild boars.

In the late 1800s and early 1900s, Eurasian wild boars were introduced to the United States in New Hampshire, New York, and North Carolina as **game animals**, or animals to be hunted. Later in the 1900s, they were also introduced as game animals to the West Coast and to some coastal islands. In some hunting preserves, all of the Eurasian wild boars were killed, but in other hunting preserves some escaped and expanded their range into surrounding forested areas.

Domestic pigs, or pigs that have been bred for captivity, also occasionally escaped to the wild and continue to do so today. Domestic pigs that live in the wild are called **feral pigs**. Feral pigs bred with the escaped Eurasian wild boars, and today very few of the descendants of Eurasian wild boars that live in the United States are pure Eurasian wild boars; most are at least part feral pig. In behavior and biology, though, the wild boars in the United States are closer to their Eurasian wild boar ancestors than to feral pigs.

Reproducing Populations of Free-Ranging Wild Boars in the United States

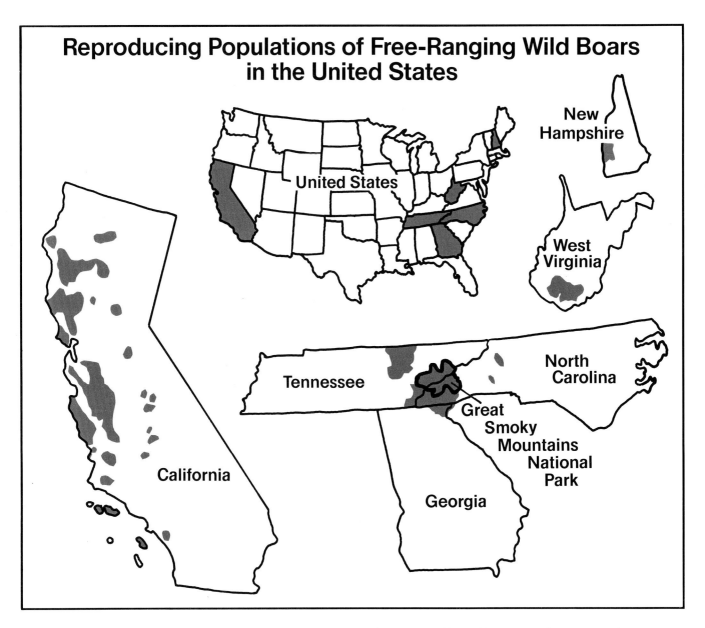

In the continental United States, groups of wild boars are now found living in wild areas in the southeastern states and California as well as in small concentrations in forests in New Hampshire. On the West Coast, the range of the wild boar continues to spread as they are illegally moved to new locations by hunters. Although they are not natural **migrators**, wild boars will move to new territories when conditions in their home range become too crowded or otherwise unfavorable.

Wild boars are amazingly adaptable animals. They can be found living in semiarid, mountainous, and forested areas around the world. Wild boars will eat almost anything found on or underneath the ground including grass, weeds, thistles, mushrooms, snails, snakes, mice, nuts, roots, insects, eggs, and **carrion**, or flesh of dead animals. On some islands in the Pacific, wild boars have even been known to catch fish and shellfish from the shallow tide waters of the ocean.

Such a variety of environments has resulted in the development of many different **subspecies**, or types, of wild boars, each having variations in their physical appearance, diet, and behavior. In Europe, wild boars generally do not grow larger than 400 pounds (181 kg), but in India, hunters have shot wild boars weighing over 800 pounds (363 kg).

The coarse **guard hairs** that make up a wild boar's outer coat of hair are black and various shades of reddish brown. Their coats turn gray with age. Young wild boars have stripes running the length of their bodies. These stripes

create shadings that blend well with the shadowy light of a forest and help hide a piglet from its enemies. Wild boar piglets keep their striped coats until they are about three months old, when the stripes begin to fade.

The head of a wild boar is long and pointed, with large ears that stand stiffly upright. Wild boars in the United States usually measure about 5 feet (1.5 m) long and have a shoulder height of about 2½ feet (.8 m). As adults, they usually weigh about 350 pounds (159 kg) but can grow to weigh over 500 pounds (227 kg), which is less than most adult domestic pigs. Unlike most domestic pigs, wild boars have straight tails.

The **canine teeth** of male wild boars

develop into long ivory **tusks** that are used as weapons and as tools for finding food. The tusks, which curve outward, have been known to grow to a length of 9 inches (23 cm). The canine teeth of female wild boars also curve into tusks, but their tusks much smaller and weaker, used mostly for digging up food rather than for fighting. The **honers**, or upper set of tusks, rub against and sharpen the **rippers**, or bottom set of tusks. Wild boars have a total of 44 teeth including the tusks.

Wild boars, except for mature males, live together in a group called a **drift** or **sounder**. A drift is usually made up of one or more **sows**, or mature female pigs, and their offspring. As soon as a male wild boar is mature and capable of breeding, when he is about a year old, he leaves the drift to live a solitary life. Although most wild boars living in a temperate climate are able to breed once or twice a year at any time during the year, they breed most often in early winter from November to January. Mature males join the drift only during mating times.

18

As part of the drift, the males fight for the right to mate with the mature females of the drift. The fighting among male wild boars is fierce. In preparation for the mating season, a plate of extra tissue, present under the hides of all males, thickens, covering the front half of both sides of their bodies. This shield can be over 2 inches (5 cm) thick and has been known to stop hunters' bullets.

Since male wild boars slash at each other's shoulders and ribs with their sharp tusks, this shield provides necessary protection. The mating season is long, but finally the males leave the drift, worn down from the fighting, to return to an independent way of life. Their shields, no longer needed, reduce in thickness.

About four months after mating, the sows in the drift **farrow**, or give birth to piglets. Shortly before farrowing, a female begins to make a farrowing nest. First the sow roots out a hole in the ground with her snout.

22

Next she lines the hole, which is large enough for her to lie down in, with mouthfuls of grass she has collected. She may then cover the grass-lined hole with a pile of sticks, creating a sort of roof structure to be covered with more grass and other plants. Such a nest will help protect the newborn piglets from the wind and damp cold of early spring, when a sow most often farrows. If available, a female wild boar will often use a natural cave or an abandoned farm building for a farrowing nest.

A wild boar sow usually farrows five or six piglets. As soon as the piglets are farrowed, they struggle to reach their mother's head. They then establish contact with her by touching their snouts to her snout. This immediate contact serves to identify each piglet to its mother and the mother to each piglet by scent. Next the newly farrowed piglets search for their mother's **teats** and begin to **nurse**, or suck milk. Each piglet seems to have one teat that it claims as its own. Scientists disagree as to the reason for this, but most think that some of the teats have more milk than others, and that there is a struggle among piglets to claim the teat with the most milk. This fighting eventually leads to the establishment of a social order that allows each piglet its own specific teat. Usually the first-farrowed piglet, having fed longer, is stronger and thus gets the teat with the most milk.

The piglets do not leave the farrowing nest until they are several days to a week old. Their mother usually does not leave them for the first few days after their birth. Then, when she must leave to forage for food, she covers the piglets with material from the nest.

When the piglets are about two weeks old, the sow will begin to take them on trips out of the farrowing nest. While they are still small, they will return to the nest to rest at some point during the day. As soon as they are taken outside the nest, the piglets begin rooting around in the ground with their snouts. They begin to eat some solid food at about two weeks of age, but their mother's

milk is their main diet until they are three months old.

Since wild boars enjoy making physical contact with each other, as do all members of the family Suidae, the piglets often lie side by side, head to toe. This helps keep the small piglets warm.

Young piglets spend much of their time playing, continuing to challenge the social order they have established while nursing. Sometimes they will play a sort of king-of-the-hill game on top of their mother.

Wild boar sows are extremely protec-tive of their young. At first, a sow with piglets does not want to be around any other wild boars except for other sows with piglets. As soon as the piglets start spending time out of the farrowing nest, though, the sow will tolerate having other young pigs around, and the drift

comes back together again.

When a wild boar sow thinks that her piglets are in danger from an intruder, she will attack viciously since the young piglets would not be able to outrun an attacker. If there are a number of adult wild boars around, they may make a circle around the piglets and face out toward the intruder with their heads lowered and the long bristles that run along the top of their backs raised to discourage an attack. An enemy will usually walk away when faced with such a threatening pose.

In the same way that wild boars of a drift will sometimes work together to defend all of their piglets, they will also work together for their common defense, even when there are no young piglets involved. When a **predator**, or an animal that kills and eats other animals, attacks and chases a drift of wild boars, sometimes the wild boars will run away in a fanlike formation. If the predator continues to chase the wild boars, the animals that are running at the opposite

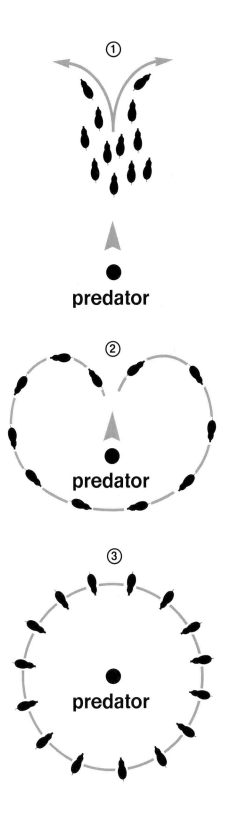

ends of the "fan" will drop back so that the predator is encircled by the drift. The wild boars, now the attackers, charge to the center of the circle to kill and then eat the luckless predator.

There are other ways that wild boars work together as a drift for their common interest. Although their vision is poor, wild boars have an excellent sense of hearing and a keen sense of smell. They have been known to smell humans from a distance of ¼ mile (402 m) away. Sometimes wild boars will follow the scent left on trees by other wild boars to determine a path likely to lead to a good source of food. Drift members may warn each other of the presence of an enemy by making a growling or snorting sound. Grunting or squealing noises express either their contentment or pain.

Wild boars also communicate through physical contact. They touch snouts in greeting and also use their snouts for grooming by rubbing them over one another's bodies to remove dirt. Wild boars are clean animals that bathe and groom often, but never so often as during the summer. They wallow in mud to protect themselves against insects and often are cleaned by fellow drift members who rub off the dried, caked mud with their snouts. Wild boars also groom themselves by rubbing up against tree trunks to remove caked dirt.

34

Throughout the summer months, wild boars spend much of the day lying in mud puddles, ponds, or streams. They must cool off in this manner because, like all pigs, they have few sweat glands. During the summer, wild boars are generally **nocturnal**, or active at night, feeding in the dark to avoid the heat of the day. If they live in an area that is close to humans, wild boars may be nocturnal throughout the year in order to avoid hunters.

As the days get cooler, wild boars usually go back to feeding mainly during the day. During the fall, there is more food for wild boars than at any other time of the year. In pastures and open fields there is plenty of hay. In oak forests there are acorns, a favorite food of wild boars, and a large number of fall seeds and berries. With hunting season in full swing during the fall, wild boars are often able to feed on dead game animals that have been shot and not found by hunters. All of this food is in addition to the insects that the wild boars root out of the ground and out of tree stumps with their snouts throughout most of the year. While rooting around in the ground, wild boars also eat some soil and certain kinds of rocks from which they get minerals and other nutrients.

The wild boars' digging and rooting for food has an effect on the plants in a forest. When wild boars root around and dig, the soil is loosened, and new seeds of trees easily take root. Wild boars often eat many of one kind of tree seed, such as acorns from oak trees, therefore decreasing the chances of these seeds taking root. Eventually, if other kinds of tree seeds take root in the turned-up soil, these new trees may take over, changing the whole forest. Wild boars' digging sometimes causes problems such as **soil erosion**, or the wearing away of the top layer of soil.

For wild boars that live in areas with cold winters, the end of fall brings new challenges. As fall turns into winter, ponds and small streams, which are wild boars' main water sources, begin to freeze. For the rest of the winter, the wild boars will eat ice and snow to get water. When the water begins to freeze, the sows of a drift begin to make a winter shelter. They dig a hole large enough for the whole drift to lie in and line it with grass. If there is a cave or an abandoned building available, the drift will use that for shelter. Drifts of wild boars are larger during the early months of winter, since this is when male wild boars join the drift to breed.

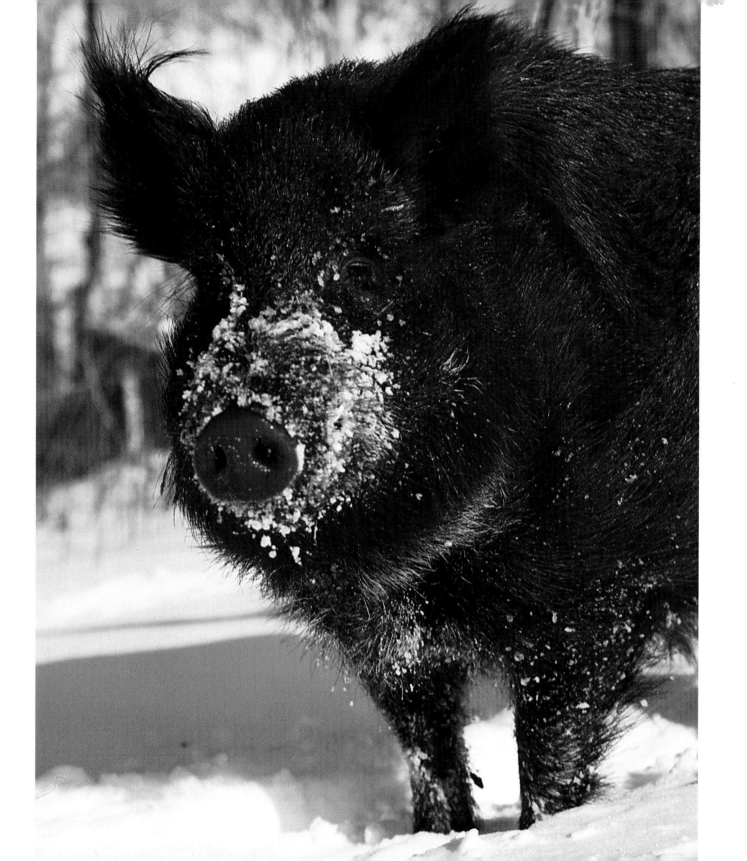

During the winter, the drift will lie huddled close together in their hole or shelter for warmth at night, leaving it to find food during the day. Wild boars living in cold climates are protected from the cold by a fatty layer of skin that is about 2 inches (5 cm) thick. A thick layer of soft hair and a coarse outer coat of longer guard hairs cover the skin.

Food is hard to find during the winter. Since the ground is frozen, wild boars must root through the snow to find small tree shoots and any surface foods, such as seeds and grass, that might be left from the fall. In addition to rooting through the snow, wild boars will strip the bark from trees with their tusks and eat the insects that might be wintering there.

As the wild boars use up the food supply close to their winter shelter, they must roam farther and farther from the shelter to search for food. The male wild boar, searching for food alone even though he has temporarily joined the drift for the breeding season, often creates a trail through the deep snow that will be used by the entire drift.

When the frozen ponds and streams begin to thaw in the spring, the wild boars' search for food becomes easier. New plants and grass sprout, and the ground thaws, allowing the wild boars to dig for roots and insects. Sometimes the melting snow will uncover an animal that has died during the winter, and the wild boars will eat that too. As the

days get warmer, animals come out of **hibernation**, or winter rest. Since the animals are still sluggish, they are easy for wild boars to catch and eat. One such animal is the snake. The bite of a snake cannot pierce a wild boar's thick hide, so even poisonous snakes may make a meal for a wild boar.

Wild boars have very few natural predators in the United States; wolves, alligators, and mountain lions are among the few wild animals that will kill and eat wild boars. Humans are the main enemy of the wild boar. Hunting for sport and professional animal control has become increasingly important to regulate the numbers of wild boars worldwide. This is especially true in areas where the wild boar has no natural predators left.

In the United States, scientists disagree on the amount of damage caused by the rooting and digging of wild boars. It is likely, though, that without control, the population of wild boars could increase so that their rooting and digging habits would noticeably change the natural environment and perhaps damage farm crops as well. Wild boars in the Great Smoky Mountains National Park in Tennessee and North Carolina cause erosion by rooting up trails and recreation areas, and they also compete with native wildlife for food, which can be scarce. For reasons such as these, wild boars are often trapped and moved to new locations where they will cause

less strain on the plants and other animals of that area.

The presence of wild boars in the

United States is an interesting example of human interference in the balance of nature. Although not originally found in the United States wild boars have adapted well to life in this land, and it seems that they are here to stay.

GLOSSARY

breed: to produce offspring by mating

canine teeth: pointed teeth toward the front of the mouths of most mammals

carrion: flesh of a dead animal

domestic pig: a pig that has been bred for captivity

drift: a group of wild boars that usually consists of sows and their offspring

family: a scientific grouping of related animals or plants

farrow: to give birth to piglets

feral pig: a domestic pig that has returned to the wild

game animal: a wild animal that is hunted for sport or food

guard hairs: long, coarse hairs in an animal's coat that protect the softer, thicker layer of hair underneath

hibernation: to pass the winter in an inactive state. During hibernation all body functions slow down.

honers: the set of tusks that protrude from a wild boar's upper jaw

migrate: to move to a new living area, usually seasonally, for feeding or breeding

nocturnal: active during the night

nurse: to suck the mother's milk

predator: an animal that kills other animals for its food

rippers: the set of tusks that protrude from a wild boar's lower jaw

soil erosion: a process by which soil is worn away

species: a group of animals or plants that share similar characteristics

sounder: another name for a drift

sow: an adult female pig

subspecies: animals or plants of the same species that have slight physical differences that are the result of adaptations to different geographical regions

teat: the tip of a female mammal's udder or breast from which milk is drawn

tusk: an elongated tooth that curves outward from a tusked animal's mouth

INDEX

adaptability, 13-14, 41
appearance: of adults 14, 16-17, 41;
   of piglets: 14-15

breeding, 6, 8, 18-20, 39, 42

coat, 14-15, 29, 41
communication, 24, 33-34

diet. *See* feeding behavior.
digging. *See* rooting.
distribution, 7, 8-13; map of, 12
domestic pigs, 10, 16
drift, 18, 20, 28-34, 39-41, 42

ecological problems, 38, 44-45
enemies, 44; defenses against, 6, 29-33
Eurasian wild boars, 8-10

farrowing, 22-24. *See also* shelter.
feeding behavior: of adults, 13, 17, 31,
   37-38, 39-43; of piglets, 24, 26-27
feral pigs, 10
fighting, 6, 17; in defense, 29-31;
   for mates, 20; of piglets, 24

grooming, 34

intelligence, 5, 6
interaction with humans, 5, 10-12,
   44-45

males, 8, 17, 18-20, 39, 42
mating. *See* breeding.

piglets, 14-15, 22, 23, 24-29

rooting, 5, 22, 26, 38, 39, 44.
   See also feeding behavior.

scientific classification: family 8, 27;
   species 8; subspecies, 14
seasonal behavior: fall, 37; spring, 42-
   43; summer, 34-36; winter, 39-42
senses, 5, 6, 33
shelter: for farrowing, 22-26;
   for winter, 39-41, 42
sow, 17, 18, 22-29, 39

tusks, 17

ABOUT THE AUTHOR

Darrel Nicholson, a graduate of the University of Minnesota, has taught at rural, suburban, and city schools. In 1967 he cofounded the Finn Creek Open Air Museum, a Finnish-American historical farm near New York Mills, Minnesota. Mr. Nicholson has been researching and studying wild boars since 1979. The photographs for *Wild Boars* were taken at a farm near his home in New York Mills.

ABOUT THE PHOTOGRAPHER

Craig Blacklock began taking photographs at a very young age under the direction of his father, photographer Les Blacklock. Craig's nature photography has illustrated several books as well as a number of fine calenders and posters. Craig and his wife, Nadine, team-teach nature photography and photography essay workshops at the Split Rock Arts Program of the University of Minnesota. The Blacklocks live in Moose Lake, Minnesota.